# Handy Iowa Genealogy Handbook

I0439900

## Gary L. Morris

©2015 Gary L. Morris

ISBN-13: 978-1508430483

ISBN-10: 1508430489

Table of Contents

# Notes

## Genealogical Research in Iowa

Tracing your family history in Iowa can be a fascinating trip through time. Locating the relevant genealogical records you'll need to find your ancestors however can be a frustrating experience. To help you avoid those frustrations when tracing your Iowa ancestry, we'll show you which records you'll need, and help you to understand:

1. What they are
2. Where to find them
3. How to use them

These records can be found both online and off, so we'll introduce you to online websites, indexes and databases, as well as brick-and-mortar repositories and other institutions that will help with your research in Iowa. So that you will have a more comprehensive understanding of these records, we have provided a brief history of the "Hawkeye State" to illustrate what type of records may have been generated during specific time periods. That information will assist you in pinpointing times and locations on which to focus the search for your Iowa ancestors and their records.

## A Brief History of Iowa

It is believed that the first Europeans to set foot in Iowa were the French explorers Louis Joliet and Father Jacques Marquette who stepped ashore where the Iowa and Missouri Rivers meet in 1673. The area was loosely governed by the French and Spanish, but was ceded to the United States in the Louisiana Purchase in 1803. Before that time as many as seventeen Native American tribes called the land their home, though most would sell it to the Federal Government of the United States by the mid-nineteenth century.

In 1829 the federal government informed two very powerful tribes living in the Illinois area, the Sauk and Mesquaki, that that would have to abandon their land and move into Iowa. The Indians made the move, albeit begrudgingly, and in 1832 the Sauk chief, Black Hawk returned to claim his former village. This sparked the Black Hawk War which lasted about three months and saw the Indians being defeated and having to relinquish some of the land they had been given in Iowa.

American settlements began to appear in the 1830,s as settlers flocked from New York, Pennsylvania, Ohio, Kentucky, Indiana, and Virginia and established farmsteads. It wasn't until the advent of the railroad in the 1860's that Iowa began to prosper economically. The railroads also brought changes to the industrial sector in Iowa. Many of the new industries that developed were agriculture related, and processing and meat packing plants began to spring up, the most famous being the Quaker Oats processing plant in Cedar Rapid.

Iowa achieved statehood in 1846 and continued to attract settlers. After nearly 30 years of peaceful development however, Iowans lives were greatly altered with the outbreak of the Civil War in 1861. There were no battles fought on Iowa soil, but the state paid a high price through the contributions of its fighting men. More than 75,000 Iowa men joined the union forces and went on to serve with distinction in the war. Of the 75,000 men who fought un the war 13,001 died, many of disease rather than killed in battle.

## Important Dates in Iowa History

**1673** - French explorers enter Iowa
**1762** - Ceded to Spain
**1788** - First white settlement established but abandoned in 1810
**1800-** Land was returned to France
**1803** - United States acquires area as part of the Louisiana Purchase
**1808** - Fort Madison built by the United States Army. Iowa included in the Illinois Territory
**1812** - Becomes Part of the Missouri Territory
**1831** - Indian tribes moved to Iowa from Illinois
**1832** - Black Hawk War
**1833** -First permanent white settlements made in eastern Iowa
**1834** - Congress attaches area to the Michigan Territory
**1836** - Iowa transferred to Wisconsin Territory
**1838** - Iowa Territory established
**1846** - Becomes a state
**1867** - First railroad built from the Mississippi River to Council Bluffs

### Famous Battles Fought in Iowa

There were no battles fought in Iowa during the Civil War, and only a few skirmishes during the Black Hawk War. The most notable Black Hawk skirmishes were the **Battle of Wisconsin Heights**, and the **Battle of Bad Axe**. The battle accounts can be very effective in uncovering the military records of your ancestor. They can tell you what regiments fought in which battles, and often include the names and ranks of many officers and enlisted men.

**Battle of Wisconsin Heights**:
http://www.wisconsinhistory.org/teachers/lessons/secondary/dodge.asp

**Battle of Bad Axe**:
http://www.wisconsinhistory.org/teachers/lessons/secondary/atkinson.asp

**Common Iowa Genealogical Issues and Resources to Overcome Them**

**Boundary Changes**: Boundary changes are a common obstacle when researching Iowa ancestors. You could be searching for an ancestor's record in one county when in fact it is stored in a different one due to historical county boundary changes. The **Atlas of Historical County Boundaries** can help you to overcome that problem. It provides a chronological listing of every boundary change that has occurred in the history of Iowa.

**Atlas of Historical County Boundaries**:
http://publications.newberry.org/ahcbp/documents/IA_Consolidated_Chronology.htm#Consolidated_Chronology

**Name Changes**: Surname changes, variations, and misspellings can complicate genealogical research. It is important to check all spelling variations. Soundex, a program that indexes names by sound, is a useful first step, but you can't rely on it completely as some name variations result in different Soundex codes. The surnames could be different, but the first name may be different too. You can also find records filed under initials, middle names, and nicknames as well, so you will need to **get creative with surname variations** and spellings in order to cover all the possibilities. For help with surname variations read our instructional article on **How to Use Soundex**.

**get creative with surname variations**:
http://obituarieshelp.org/blog/?p=634

**How to Use Soundex**: http://obituarieshelp.org/blog/?p=505

## Iowa Genealogical Organizations and Archives

Genealogical resources include not only records, but the organizations that house them, or can direct you to them. These institutions include: *Archives, Libraries, Genealogical Societies, Family History Centers, Universities, Churches, and Museums.*

Following are links to their websites, their physical addresses, and a summary of the records you can find there.

Iowa Archives

**National Archives at Kansas City** - naturalization records, Native American records, census records, and immigration records

400 West Pershing Road
Kansas City, MO 64108.
Phone: 816-268-8000
E-mail: **kansascity.archives@nara.gov**

**National Archives at Kansas City** link to:
http://www.archives.gov/kansas-city/

**Iowa Public Library** - Census records, maps, city directories, military records

123 South Linn Street
Iowa City, IA 52240
319.356.5200
Tel:319.887.6004
Email: maeve-clark@icpl.org

**Iowa Public Library**: http://www.icpl.org/local-history/

**University of Iowa Digital Library** – manuscripts, historic newspapers, historical maps, ethnic and women's histories

**University of Iowa Digital Library**: http://digital.lib.uiowa.edu/

Iowa Genealogical and Historical Societies

Genealogical and historical societies have access to extensive catalogues of genealogical data. They are also able to offer expert guidance for genealogical researchers. Many members are professional genealogists who are most willing to share their expertise in finding ancestors.

**Iowa Genealogical Society** – census, vital records, religious records, city directories, military records, family histories

6000 Douglas Ave.
P.O. Box 7735
Des Moines, IA 50322
Telephone: 515-276-0287

**Iowa Genealogical Society**: http://iowagenealogy.org/

**Old Fort Genealogical Society** – cemetery records, township maps, old settlers list

Ft Madison Public Library
1920 Ave E
Ft Madison, IA 52627

**Old Fort Genealogical Society**:
http://freepages.genealogy.rootsweb.ancestry.com/~oldfort/

**State Historical Society of Iowa** (State Archives) - land records, military records, family histories

600 East Locust
Des Moines, Iowa 50319
515-281-5111

**State Historical Society of Iowa**:
http://www.iowahistory.org/index.html

**Additional Iowa Genealogical Resources**

Iowa Mailing Lists

Mailing lists are internet based facilities that use email to distribute a single message to all who subscribe to it. When information on a particular surname, new records, or any other important genealogy information related to the mailing list topic becomes available, the subscribers are alerted to it. Joining a mailing list is an excellent way to stay up to date on Iowa genealogy research topics. Rootsweb have an extensive listing of **Iowa Mailing Lists** on a variety of topics.

**Iowa Mailing Lists**:
http://lists.rootsweb.ancestry.com/index/usa/IA/misc.html

Iowa Message Boards

A message board is another internet based facility where people can post questions about a specific genealogy topic and have it answered by other genealogists. If you have questions about a surname, record type, or research topic, you can post your question and other researchers and genealogists will help you with the answer. Be sure to check back regularly, as the answers are not emailed to you. The Iowa message boards at **Rootsweb** are completely free to use.

**Rootsweb**:
http://boards.rootsweb.com/localities.northam.usa.states/mb.ashx

Iowa Newspapers and Periodicals

Many genealogy periodicals and historical newspapers contain reprinted copies of family genealogies, transcripts of family Bible records, information about local records and archives, census indexes, church records, queries, land records, obituaries, court records, cemetery records, and wills. The following sites have historical Iowa newspapers and periodicals that you can search online or on-site.

**State Historical Society of Iowa** (State Archives) – historic books, periodicals, historical newspapers from 1836 to present

600 East Locust
Des Moines, Iowa 50319
515-281-5111

**State Historical Society of Iowa**:
http://www.iowahistory.org/shsi/libraries/index.html

**University of Iowa Digital Library** – miscellaneous historical newspapers

**University of Iowa Digital Library**: http://digital.lib.uiowa.edu/

**Newspaper Archives of Plymouth County** – searchable online index of historical Iowa newspapers dating from the 19th century

**Newspaper Archives of Plymouth County**:
http://plymouthcounty.newspaperarchive.com/

**GenealogyBank.com** – free searchable database of Iowa newspaper archives, 1837–1900

**GenealogyBank.com**:
http://www.genealogybank.com/gbnk/newspapers/explore/USA/Iowa/

**Library of Congress Digital Newspaper Directory** – free searchable database of historical U.S. newspapers dating from 1690-present

**Library of Congress Digital Newspaper Directory**: http://chroniclingamerica.loc.gov/search/titles/

**The Online Books Page** – links to historical books and periodicals available for viewing online, dating from mid-16<sup>th</sup> century

**The Online Books Page**: http://onlinebooks.library.upenn.edu

**NewspaperArchive.com** – largest online database of historical newspapers in the world.

**NewspaperArchive.com**: http://newspaperarchive.com/

Historical Iowa Maps and Gazetteers

Maps are an integral part of genealogical research. They help us to locate landmarks, towns, cities, parishes, states, provinces, waterways and roads and streets. They also help us to determine when and where boundary changes might have taken place, and give us a visualization of the area we're researching in.

For locating place names, a gazetteer is the best possible resource for any genealogist. Gazetteers are also sometimes called "place name dictionaries", and can help you to locate the area in which you need to conduct research. Below are links to the maps and gazetteers for research in Iowa.

**Peabody GNIS Service – Iowa**:
http://peabody.research.yale.edu/cgi-bin/Query.GNIS?ST=Iowa&SU=1

**Color Landform Atlas – Iowa**:
http://fermi.jhuapl.edu/states/ia_0.html

**1985 U.S. Atlas**: http://www.livgenmi.com/1895/IA/

**Iowa Hometown Locator**: http://iowa.hometownlocator.com/

Iowaa City Directories

.

City directories are similar to telephone directories in that they list the residents of a particular area. The difference though is what is important to genealogists, and that is they pre-date telephone directories. You can find an ancestor's information such as their street address, place of employment, occupation, or the name of their spouse. A one-stop-shop for finding city directories in Iowa is the **Iowa Online Historical Directories** which contains a listing of every available historical directory related to Iowa.

**Iowa Online Historical Directories**:
https://sites.google.com/site/onlinedirectorysite/Home/usa/in

**Iowa Public Library** – Wide selection of city directories on microfilm

123 South Linn Street
Iowa City, IA 52240
319.356.5200
Tel:319.887.6004
Email: maeve-clark@icpl.org

**Iowa Public Library**: http://www.icpl.org/local-history/

# Iowa Genealogical Records

Birth, Death, Marriage and Divorce Records – Also known as vital records, birth, death, and marriage certificates are the most basic, yet most important records attached to your ancestor. The reason for their importance is that they not only place your ancestor in a specific place at a definite time, but potentially connect the individual to other relatives. Below is a list of repositories and websites where you can find Iowa vital records

The **Iowa Bureau of Health Statistics** has birth, death, and marriage records starting from 1880. Records before 1880 must be acquired from individual **Iowa County Clerks** offices.

Iowa Dept. of Public Health
Bureau of Health Statistics
Lucas Office Building
321 E. 12th St., 1st Floor
Des Moines, IA 50319-0075
Phone (515) 281-4944

**Iowa Bureau of Health Statistics**:
http://www.idph.state.ia.us/apl/health_statistics.asp#vital

**Iowa County Clerks**:
http://iagenweb.org/state/research/bmdguide.htm

**Family Search** has the following indexes which can be searched online:
**Iowa Births and Christenings, 1830-1950**:
https://familysearch.org/search/collection/1674820

**Iowa, County Births, 1880-1935**:
https://familysearch.org/search/collection/1821206

**Iowa, Marriages, 1809-1992**:
https://familysearch.org/search/collection/1674842

**Iowa, Deaths and Burials, 1850-1990**:
https://familysearch.org/search/collection/1674841

Census Reports

Census records are among the most important genealogical documents for placing your ancestor in a particular place at a specific time. Like BDM records, they can also lead you to other ancestors, particularly those who were living under the authority of the head of household.

Federal census records for Iowa exist from 1840 through 1930, and can be found in the following repositories:

**National Archives at Kansas City** - census records for all states 1790-1930

400 West Pershing Road
Kansas City, MO 64108.
Phone: 816-268-8000
E-mail: kansascity.archives@nara.gov

**National Archives at Kansas City**:
http://www.archives.gov/kansas-city/

**State Historical Society of Iowa** - federal census records from 1840 through 1930, state census records for 1856, 1885, 1895, 1905, 1915 and 1925 and special census records for 1838, 1844, 1846-1847, 1849, and 1851-1854. Agricultural, industrial, mortality, and social census records are available for selected years.

600 East Locust
Des Moines, Iowa 50319
515-281-5111

**State Historical Society of Iowa**:
http://www.iowahistory.org/index.html

The **Free Census Project** has transcribed many Iowa indexes and new material is added daily

**Free Census Project**: http://usgwcensus.org/cenfiles/ia.htm

**Access Genealogy** - Iowa census records from 1820-1930

**Access Genealogy**: http://www.accessgenealogy.com/census/iowa-census-records.htm

**African American Census Schedules Online** – slave schedules, mortality schedules, slave-owners census

**African American Census Schedules Online**: http://www.afrigeneas.com/aacensus

**Native Americans in Census Records** (US National Archives)

**Native Americans in Census Records**: http://www.archives.gov/research/census/native-americans/

Iowa Church Records

Church and synagogue records are a valuable resource, especially for baptisms, marriages, and burials that took place before 1900. You will need to at least have an idea of your ancestor's religious denomination, and in most cases you will have to visit a brick and mortar establishment to view them.

Most church records are kept by the individual church, although in some denominations, records are placed in a regional archive or maintained at the diocesan level. Local Historical Societies are sometimes the repository for the state's older church records. Below are links archives that maintain church records, as well as a few databases that can be viewed online.

The **Family History Library** contains many church records from a variety of denominations on microfilm.

**Family History Library**:
http://familysearch.org/learn/wiki/en/Family_History_Library

The **Swenson Center** at Augustana College in Illinois has many Iowa Church records from Evangelical, Lutheran, Baptist, and First Covenant Churches from around the state

**Swenson Center**: http://www.augustana.edu/general-information/swenson-center-/genealogy/church-records/alabama---iowa

**Parish Baptism Registers for Trinity Episcopal Church** and in Muscatine and **Death and Baptism Records for St. Peter's Lutheran Church** in Montpelier can be found online.

**Parish Baptism Registers for Trinity Episcopal Church**:
http://www.rootsweb.ancestry.com/~iamusca2/trinity1.htm

**Death and Baptism Records for St. Peter's Lutheran Church**:
http://www.rootsweb.ancestry.com/~iamusca2/index.html

## Central Repositories for Denominational Records

Most of the records of individual denominations are kept in central repositories. Below is a list of the major congregational archives for Iowa with links to their websites, physical addresses, and contact information.

Baptist

**North American Baptist Conference**
1 South 210 Summit Avenue
Oakbrook Terrace, IL 60181
Phone: (630) 495-2000
Fax: (630) 495-0333

**North American Baptist Conference**:
http://www.nabconference.org/

Church of Jesus Christ of Latter-day Saints (Mormons)

Early records for Mormons in Iowa Wards and Branches can be found on microfilm at the LDS Family History Library in Salt Lake City. The film numbers can be searched online at the **Family History Library Catalog**

**Family History Library Catalog**:
https://familysearch.org/eng/Library/FHLC/frameset_fhlc.asp

Lutheran

**Evangelical Lutheran Church in America**
Wartburg Theological Seminary
333 Wartburg Place
Dubuque, IA 52001
Phone: (563) 589-0200 Fax: (563) 589-0333

**Evangelical Lutheran Church in America**: http://www.elca.org/

## Methodist

**Iowa Wesleyan College Library**
Mt. Pleasant, IA 52641
Phone: (319) 385-6317
Fax: (319) 385-6324

**Iowa Wesleyan College Library**: http://www.iwc.edu/

## Presbyterian

**The Presbyterian Historical Society**
425 Lombard Street
Philadelphia, PA 19147
Phone: (215) 627-1852
Fax: (215) 627-0509

**The Presbyterian Historical Society**: http://www.history.pcusa.org/

## Roman Catholic

**Diocese of Davenport**
2706 N. Gaines Street
Davenport, IA 52804
Phone: (319) 324-1911
Fax: (319) 324-5842

**Diocese of Davenport**: http://www.davenportdiocese.org/

**Diocese of Sioux City**
1821 Jackson Street
Sioux City, IA 51105
Phone: (712) 255-7933
Fax: (712) 233-7598

**Diocese of Sioux City**: http://www.scdiocese.org/

**Diocese of Des Moines**
610 Grand Avenue
Des Moines, IA 50309
Phone: (515) 243-7653
Fax: (515) 237-5070

**Diocese of Des Moines**: http://www.dmdiocese.org/

**Archdiocese of Dubuque**
Archdiocesan Center
1229 Mt Loretta Ave.
Dubuque, IA 52004-0479
Phone: (563) 556-2580

**Archdiocese of Dubuque**:
http://www.arch.pvt.k12.ia.us/Archives/index.html

Society of Friends (Quaker)

**Magill Library Haverford College**
Haverford, PA 19041-1392
Phone: (610) 896-1161
Fax: (610) 896-1102

**Magill Library Haverford College**:
http://www.haverford.edu/library/special/

Iowa Military Records

More than 40 million Americans have participated in some time of war service since America was colonized. The chance of finding your ancestor amongst those records is exceptionally high. Military records can even reveal individuals who never actually served, such as those who registered for the two World Wars but were never called to duty.

Below are a number of links to websites and archives that contain Iowa military records.

**State Historical Society of Iowa** (State Archives) – Spanish and Mexican War records, Civil War records, records of the Iowa Adjutant General from the territorial period to 1915, Grand Army of the Republic roster books and post minutes, World Wars I and II casualty lists, Iowa veterans grave registration records,

600 East Locust
Des Moines, Iowa 50319
515-281-5111

**State Historical Society of Iowa**:
http://www.iowahistory.org/index.html

**U.S. National Archives** – WWI Draft registration cards, casualties lists, WWI and WWII service records, Korean War records, Vietnam War records, Civil War and Spanish-American War records, and casualties lists.

**U.S. National Archives**:
http://www.archives.gov/research/military/veterans/online.html

**US Department of Veterans Affairs Nationwide Gravesite Locator** – includes information on veterans and their family members buried in veterans and military cemeteries having a government grave marker.

**US Department of Veterans Affairs Nationwide Gravesite Locator**: http://gravelocator.cem.va.gov/

**United States Index to Indian Wars Pension Files, 1892-1926** – military pension records of soldiers who fought in the Indian Wars between 1817 and 1898

**United States Index to Indian Wars Pension Files, 1892-1926**: https://familysearch.org/search/collection/1979427

**United States Registers of Enlistments in the U.S. Army, 1798-1914** - index of men who enlisted in the United States Army, 1798-1914.

**United States Registers of Enlistments in the U.S. Army, 1798-1914**: https://familysearch.org/search/collection/1880762

**United States Mexican War Pension Index, 1887-1926** - index to Mexican War pension files for service between 1846 and 1848

**United States Mexican War Pension Index, 1887-1926**: https://familysearch.org/search/collection/1979390

**Civil War Soldiers Service Records** - Service records for both Union and Confederate soldiers indexed by soldier's name, rank, and unit.

**Civil War Soldier Service Records**: http://go.fold3.com/civilwar_records/

Iowa Cemetery Records

As convenient as it is to search cemetery records online, keep in mind that there are a few disadvantages over visiting a cemetery in person. They are:

1. Tombstone information is not always accurately transcribed
2. The arrangement of the graves in a cemetery can be crucial as family members are often buried next to each other or in the same grave. This arrangement is not always preserved in the alphabetical indexes that are found online.

With that information in mind, the following websites have databases that can be searched online for Iowa Cemetery records.

**Iowa Tombstone Transcription Project** - death and burial records

**Iowa Tombstone Transcription Project**:
http://usgwtombstones.org/iowa/iowa.html

**African American Cemeteries Online** – African American, slave, and Native American cemetery records

**African American Cemeteries Online**:
http://africanamericancemeteries.com/

**Access Genealogy** – huge database of Iowa cemetery record transcriptions

**Access Genealogy**:
http://www.accessgenealogy.com/cemetery/iowa-cemetery-records.htm

**Find a Grave** – over 100 million grave records can be searched on this site. Search can be conducted by name, location, or cemetery name.

**Find a Grave**: http://www.findagrave.com/

**Interment.net** - A free online database containing approximately 4 million cemetery records from around the world.

**Interment.net**: http://www.interment.net/

**Billion Graves** – as the name implies, you can search a billion records including headstone photos, transcriptions, cemetery records, and grave locations.

**Billion Graves**:
http://billiongraves.com/pages/search/index.php#cemetery

Iowa Obituaries

Obituaries can reveal a wealth about our ancestor and other relatives. You can search our **Iowa Newspaper Obituaries Listings** from hundreds of Iowa newspapers online for free.

**Iowa Newspaper Obituaries Listings**:
http://obituarieshelp.org/iowa_newspaper_obituaries.html

## Iowa Wills and Probate Records

The documents found in a probate packet may include a complete inventory of a person's estate, newspaper entries, witness testimony, a copy of a will, list of debtors and creditors, names of executors or trustees, names of heirs. They can not only tell you about the ancestor you're currently researching, but lead to other ancestors. Most of these records must be accessed at a county court or clerk's office, but some can be found online as well. You can obtain copies of the original probate records by writing to the county clerk.

Iowa probate records exist since around 1834. They can be found at individual **Iowa Clerks of the District Court** where you can request copies of wills, administrations, dockets, calendars, and other records

**Iowa Clerks of the District Court**:
http://www.iowacourts.gov/About_the_Courts/District_Courts/

The Family History Library has microfilmed probate records for Iowa. They can be searched for in the **Family History Library Catalogue** as IOWA-PROBATE RECORDS

**Family History Library Catalogue**:
https://familysearch.org/eng/Library/FHLC/frameset_fhlc.asp

## Iowa Immigration and Naturalization Records

The naturalization process generated many types of records, including petitions, declarations of intention, and oaths of allegiance. These records can provide family historians with information such as a person's birth date and place of birth, immigration year, marital status, spouse information, occupation, witnesses' names and addresses, and more.

As Iowa has no ports, many of those who arrived in Iowa came via the East Coast ports such as New York, Boston, or Philadelphia. Most immigrants to the area were pioneers who came overland. The Iowa Genealogical Society has a searchable online index of **Pioneer Certificates**, dating from the early 1800's- 2003. Pioneer Certificates are issued to those who can prove they are directly descended from original Iowa pioneers. The value in this collection is that it provides the name of the original pioneer, and the collection also includes family genealogies, marriage records, wills, and land records.

**Pioneer Certificates**: http://iowagenealogy.org/?page_id=55

**US National Archives** – Immigration and Naturalization records for the entire United States, Passenger Lists

**US National Archives**:
http://www.archives.gov/research/immigration/passenger-arrival.html

Iowa Native American Records

**Iowa Genealogical Society Library** – records containing the census of the Sac & Fox Indians of the Mississippi living at the settlement in Tama, Iowa covering the period from 1891 – 1939 as well as a multitude of Native American research resources

**Iowa Genealogical Society Library**:
http://www.iowapioneers.com/Library/NaAmRsrc2.htm

**Access Genealogy** – Iowa Native American census records, tribal histories, and much more

**Access Genealogy**: http://www.accessgenealogy.com/native/iowa-indian-tribes.htm

**U.S. National Archives** - information on American Indians who maintained their ties to Federally-recognized Tribes (1830-1970).

**U.S. National Archives**: http://www.archives.gov/research/native-americans/

**Records of the Bureau of Indian Affairs (BIA)** link to:
http://www.archives.gov/research/guide-fed-records/groups/075.html

**American Indians Records Repository** - records dating from the 1700s including trust, education and other historic Indian Affairs records

American Indian Records Repository
Meritex Enterprises
17501 West 98th Street
Lenexa, KS 66219
Phone: 913-888-0601

**American Indians Records Repository**:
http://www.doi.gov/ost/records_mgmt/american-indian-records-repository.cfm

# Missing Matriarchs – Resources for Researching Female Iowa Ancestors

Looking for female ancestors requires an adjustment of how we view traditional records sources. A woman's identity was often under that of her husband, and often individual records for them can be difficult to locate. The following resources are effective in locating female ancestors in Iowa where traditional records may not reveal them.

Marriage and Divorce Records

County clerks began recording marriages in 1834, and state-wide registration commenced in 1880. The Iowa State Department of Health in Des Moines has indexed these records from 1919. Divorce registration began in 1906 and has been under the jurisdiction of the county district and chancery courts.

The **State Historical Society of Iowa** has county marriage records dating from 1835-1934, and state records from 1880-1920.

**State Historical Society of Iowa**:
http://www.iowahistory.org/index.html

You can find divorce records dating from 1835-1950 at the Des Moines County Courthouse (film 1547826 ff.)

Bibliographies

- *Open Country, Iowa: Rural Women, Tradition, and Change,* Deborah Fink (State University of New York Press, 1986)
- *Remarkable Iowa Women,* Ethel W. Hanft (River Bend Publishing, 1983)
- *The Blue Book of Iowa Women: A History of Contemporary Women,* Winona Evans Reeves (W. C. Cox and Co. 1974)

## Selected Resources for Iowa Women's History

Amana Heritage Society
PO Box 81
Amana, IA 52203

Iowa Women's Archives
University of Iowa Library
100 Main Library
Iowa City, IA 52242

**University of Iowa Digital Library** – miscellaneous women's history records and other resources

**University of Iowa Digital Library**: http://digital.lib.uiowa.edu/

## Common Iowa Surnames

The following surnames are among the most common in Iowa and are also being currently researched by other genealogists. If you find your surname here, there is a chance that some research has already been performed on your ancestor.

Adair, Adams, Allamakee, Appanoose, Audubon, Benton, BlackHawk, Boone, Bremer, Buchanan, BuenaVista, Butler, Calhoun, Carroll, Cass, Cedar, CerroGordo, Cherokee, Chickasaw, Clarke, Clay, Clayton, Clinton, Crawford, Dallas, Davis, Decatur, Delaware, DesMoines, Dickinson, Dubuque, Emmet, Fayette, Floyd, Franklin, Fremont, Greene, Grundy, Guthrie, Hamilton, Hancock, Hardin, Harrison, Henry, Howard, Humboldt, Ida, Iowa, Jackson, Jasper, Jefferson, Johnson, Jones, Keokuk, Kossuth, Lee, Linn, Louisa, Lucas, Lyon, Madison, Mahaska, Marion, Marshall, Mills, Mitchell, Monona, Monroe, Montgomery, Muscatine, Obrien, Osceola, Page, PaloAlto, Plymouth, Pocahontas, Polk, Pottawattamie, Poweshiek, Ringgold, Sac, Scott, Shelby, Sioux, Story, Tama, Taylor, Union, VanBuren, Wapello, Warren, Washington, Wayne, Webster, Winnebago, Winneshiek, Woodbury, Worth, Wright

About the Author

Gary L. Morris worked from 2009 to 2014 as a professional researcher for a major player in the genealogy field. After tracing his family lineage back to 1683, he found that genealogy could be an expensive undertaking. As such, has decided to publish these helpful guides to share the valuable free information he has discovered during his career to help others trace their family lineages as inexpensively as possible. An avid genealogist himself, he hopes you will find this guide factual, thorough, helpful, and most of all, effective in helping you to find your family members.

# Notes

# Notes

www.ingramcontent.com/pod-product-compliance
Lightning Source LLC
Chambersburg PA
CBHW071343310526
45790CB00018B/1267